fundamentals
for
men

A HANDBOOK FOR HIM

VINCE MILLER

RESOLUTE

fundamentals
for
Men

First Edition: 2020
Fundamentals For Men: A Handbook For Him / Vince Miller
Paperback ISBN: 978-1-951304-38-6
eBook ISBN: 978-1-951304-39-3

EQUIP PRESS

Colorado Springs

TO:

FROM:

CONTENTS

HOW TO USE THIS HANDBOOK

VIDEOS FOR THIS HANDBOOK

As you navigate this handbook, you will discover that the lessons are designed for use with online videos. These videos are viewable with a membership at our website: **www.beresolute.org**. You can use the videos for individual growth or with a group of men. Each lesson corresponds with the video of the same title. The best part is Vince Miller has structured the videos to provide relevant content for reflection and discussion, so that you don't need hours to prepare. He does the work for you. Just push *play* on the video, and then reference this handbook.

THE METHOD

We believe in providing men with a full-scale game plan for growth. We are not just giving you content, but a *method* that has been field-tested with hundreds of thousands of men. While choosing the material is essential, we believe our step by step process is one of the best for producing a spiritual change in a man's life. We have tested the components in each session and how they link together within a series or group of series that complement a man's ongoing growth. Our goal is to produce life change. In each lesson, you will notice clear goals and outcomes, purposeful reflection and discussion questions, a rich study of God's Word, and practical application with actionable steps to be taken. While we know men need content, we hope our commitment to this method deepens their relationship with Christ and with one another.

THERE IS MORE IN THIS SERIES

Remember, once you finish this series, there are many others that follow it and build upon it. Don't do just one series, do them all!

HOW TO LEAD MEN

ONE | GATHER YOUR TEAM

Assembling a team is critical. A team should include a pair of leaders who become the "On-Site Hosts" for the experience. We believe working in pairs is by far the most practical approach. Remember, every pilot needs a wingman.

TWO | RECRUIT MEN

Don't stress: whether you recruit half a dozen men or a hundred, the content will be useful. We have found the best recruiting success comes from finding men who are hungry to grow spiritually. While the content is suitable for any believer of any age, the best recruit is the one who wants to be there, a man who hungers for the Word of God, and occasionally some food as well!

THREE | MAKE SURE EACH MAN HAS A HANDBOOK

Our guides may be purchased in the online store: www.beresolute.org. These are your guides for taking notes, guiding a dialogue with men in your group, and recording outcomes at the end of every lesson. Handbooks also include other materials for additional development. You will want one for each lesson series.

FOUR | ONLINE RESOURCES FOR LEADERS

If you have purchased online video access with your membership, you can view all the material. You will be able to listen to audio recaps, watch the videos, read the full transcripts, and even review past lessons. There are also training articles and videos online to help you lead your group.

FIVE | **MORE MATERIAL & VINCE MILLER**

At Resolute, we are not just providing content. We are inviting you to an experience. Here are other tools you can utilize.

- Need a devotional? Read the Men's Daily Devotional: www.beresolute.org/mdd
- Need prayer? Vince Miller will personally pray for you: www.beresolute.org
- Need a speaker? Invite Vince Miller to speak: beresolute.org/vince-miller
- Need help as a men's leader? Contact Vince Miller directly at vince@beresolute.org

It is our goal to partner with you and your men's ministry. We want to resource you with tools that compliment your development as a man of God and as a leader.

SIX | **CONNECT SOCIALLY**

We would love to have you join our social networks. Head to our home page and connect with us on Twitter, LinkedIn, and Facebook.

ABOUT VINCE MILLER

Vince Miller was born in Vallejo, California, and grew up on the West Coast. At twenty, he made a profession of faith while in college and felt a strong, sudden call to work in full-time ministry. After college and graduate school, he invested two decades working with notable ministries like Young Life, InterVarsity Christian Fellowship, the local church, and in senior interim roles. He currently lives in St. Paul, Minnesota, with his wife Christina and their three teenage children.

In March 2014, he founded Resolute out of his passion for discipleship and leadership development of men. This passion was born out of his personal need for growth. Vince turned everywhere to find a man who would mentor, disciple, and develop him throughout his spiritual life. He often received two answers from well-meaning Christian leaders: *either they did not know what to do in a mentoring relationship, or they simply did not have the time to do it.* Vince learned that he was not alone. Many Christian men were seeking this type of mentorship relationship. Therefore, he felt compelled to build an organization that would focus on two things: ensuring that men who want to be discipled have the opportunity and that they have real tools to disciple other men.

Vince is an authentic and transparent leader who loves to communicate with men and has a deep passion for God's Word. He has authored several books, and he is the primary content creator of all Resolute content and training materials.

A PERSONAL NOTE FROM VINCE

I pray this experience will benefit your life and your spiritual journey as a man. I hope you will do three things as you engage.

First, that you will be receptive to the Word of God. I love that we dig into the Bible every time we meet. The Bible is not an afterthought in Resolute—it is the means of discovering God and transformation.

Second, lean into the brotherhood of this experience. Build friendships, share transparently, and have conversations that go beyond the superficial.

Third, apply what you have learned. Take an action item with you every week, knowing that one small step weekly leads to success over a lifetime.

Keep moving forward,

Vince Miller

INTRODUCTION

Gentlemen, welcome. I am excited to be with you.

In this series, entitled Fundamentals, we are going to be looking at topics that I believe are fundamental to the spiritual development of men in their Christian faith. Now I think some men dismiss a series like this thinking it's too rudimentary and maybe not deep enough for them. But that again misunderstands what it looks like to go deeper in our faith. Often a deeper, richer, and more profound faith in Christ is found in taking fundamental activities further. I know in my work with men, I have found that the topics in this series are one's that men come back to time and time again. So whether you are new Christian or old one for that matter, these topics will bless your Christian life.

I remember years ago, Michael Jordon said something on this point, that stuck with me forever. He said,

---

"You can practice shooting eight hours a day, but if your technique is wrong, then all you become is very good at shooting the wrong way. Get the fundamentals down, and the level of everything you do will rise."

This was the genius of Jordan. He took fundamental techniques and scaled them up and made them look superhuman. But at the core, they were fundamental.

I would say this principle is biblical, timeless, and applicable in our faith as well. Just listen to what God says to Joshua.

This Book of the Law shall not depart from your mouth, but you shall meditate on it day and night, so that you may be careful to do according to all that is written in it. For then you will make your way prosperous, and then you will have good success.

Joshua 1:8

God keeps this very fundamental for Joshua. Here's what he says. Speak it. Think about it. Do it. This will lead to your spiritual prosperity and success. That's it. Fundamental!

So, in this study, we are going to dig into and dig out some fundamentals that I believe we as men need to master in all parts of our life.

FUNDAMENTAL

1

INDUCTIVE BIBLE STUDY

We are going to begin by learning how to read and study the Bible.

Since I have been a pastor and teacher for almost three decades, I believe the greatest gift you can give any man is the ability to read, study, and understand the Bible. Because the Bible is the most incredible discipleship tool we have. I believe if you can teach a man how to read, study, and understand the Bible, then he can, on his own, extract a lifetime of principles from it. Yet, I believe most Christian men have a hard time drawing truth from it and therefore don't turn to it when we need it most.

Goal

The goal in today's lesson is to share with you one of the oldest approaches to reading, studying, and understanding your Bible. Teachers and pastors have used it for hundreds of years. Our goal is to get you into the Bible this week, throughout this study, and hopefully for the rest of your life.

Pray

God, be with us today as men and as we approach your truth, and as we dig into spiritual principles for reading your Word. Give us discernment and sharp minds as we listen to you speak and act on what we learn. In Christ's name—Amen.

Opener Reflection Questions
- How often do you read the Bible?
- What is intimidating about reading the Bible?
- Do you feel like you understand the Bible more when you hear it taught? Why or why not?

The Inductive Bible Study Method

I'm going to walk you through a simple bible study method that many refer to as the Inductive Bible Study Method.

The word inductive refers to a process we use to read and understand any form of literature; in this case we are talking about the Bible. This is because there are two common ways to read and reason. One is called inductive, and the other is called deductive.

Inductive Reasoning seeks to draw meaning out of specifics and then make a general conclusion. **Deductive Reasoning** aims to reach a conclusion and then prove the specifics. Men tend to read the Bible is deductively, but this leads to us importing our ideas, opinions, and experiences into the Bible, which can lead to errors. However, if we can read the Bible inductively, drawing from the specifics of the text and letting it speak for itself, we will both remain faithful to God's intended meaning and discover the best application for life change. The Bible is a spiritual book with spiritual implications. As we read, we have to remember that we are the ones who are changed by God's unchanging Word.

So, let me walk you through the inductive process in three simple steps:

The first step is **Observation**.

Observation is the step that too many men fly past but shouldn't. Here we are looking at **what the text says.** This means we have to take time looking at the raw content. I find a section of scripture (typically a paragraph or two) and read it multiple times, observing what the text says (Note: not what it says to *me*, just what the text is saying). While I am reading, I am persistently scanning the text for the following six things while I am trying to figure out what the text says. I usually start by looking for some of the smallest details and then, along the way, discover the larger details.

First, I am looking at the **Words**. I know this seems basic, but when I look at the words, I am identifying the people, places, or things in the text. I am also noticing the central or repeated words that bring attention to the subject and theme.

Second, I am looking for **Characters**. Taking a small step back from the words, I want to make sure I am familiar with the people or characters in the text and the activity taking place around them.

Third, I'm looking at the **Grammar**. Another small step back, and I am starting to identify the subject, the verb, and the object of the text. I am trying to determine what words and characters take center stage. For example, I may occasionally notice the use of contrasts and comparisons that repeat. If so, these are emphasizing something I need to give attention to.

Fourth, I am looking at sentence **Structure**. I want to examine how sentences and paragraphs come together. I am looking for connecting phrases like the word "*therefore.*" Words like *therefore* tell us to pay attention to previous statements, and that a resultant thought is coming.

Fifth, I want to be aware of the **Genre**. Yes, a little bit of a fancy word, but this means I need to note the type of literature I am reading. We always need to pay attention to the kind of text we're reading: whether it's poetry, prose, letter, narrative, or prophetic literature. This helps us to define the context of the greater story.

Sixth, and finally, I want to note the **Mood** of the text. Here I notice the tone of the text by paying attention to the actions and emotions of the writer and the audience to whom it was written.

I am always looking for these same six things. The more you practice looking for them, the more proficient you will be, which will lead you to see more in the text, which leads to better observations. I think this is precisely why people who read the Bible for years still discover more and more truth from a single section of scripture and thus have a more in-depth experience with God's Word. This is what makes fundamentals so great.

When I am leading others in a Bible study, I spend most of my time asking men what they observe in the text. I would suggest spending most of your time here. The key to making the very best observations is to avoid doing two things that disrupt the process. First, avoid asking the question, "What does this mean to me?" Which is a question of interpretation and not an observation. Second, avoid making comments that begin with "Here is what this means to me…" Which again is not an observation; it is called making an application. If you avoid these two pitfalls (which are the next steps) and spend more time making observations, and good ones, then your questions of interpretation will be answered, and your comments on the application will be stronger.

Step two: Interpretation.

Here we are trying to discern one thing, and that is what the text meant, not to us, but "What it meant to them." Now it's okay to ask any question of interpretation that we have been trying not to do in step one. This is an important question because the Bible was not written to us, even though it's for us. Yep: it was not written to you at all. Forty different authors wrote it over a span of 2000 years, each book had an original audience. Now, this does not mean that the book does not have application for us today, but simply that we first must recognize the intent of writing to them in their day. The first audience of every book in the Bible is the people group to whom it was written. In the interpretation stage, we're looking to find the author's intended meaning to that audience. So, what I like to do here is think of myself as an investigative reporter: the good kind of reporter, one that asks reporter-style questions. Questions like, who, what, where, when, how, and why. Questions like this dig after the historical context, and most of them are answered from the observations we made in the last step. Once in a while, I may need a little bit of historical help. Therefore, sometimes I turn to a Study Bible to get a better understanding of the context. But what we are trying to do is discover the one main point the author is trying to drive home to his audience, and what we are trying to avoid is importing our cultural assumptions into the text, which can lead us to make the wrong interpretation, and thus incorrect application.

Finally, the third big step is Application.

Application is where I am trying to find how the interpretation connects to my everyday life. I am usually thinking about two questions. What challenges am I currently facing that the text addressed? What steps do I need to take based on observation and interpretation? I base the answers to these two questions on all I have discovered in my observations and interpretations.

I'll tell you, I have used this process for years and find it be illuminating whether I am engaging in personal study, preparing for a sermon, or studying with a group of men. I memorize this process with the acronym O.I.A. which stands for Observation, Interpretation, and Application.

Trying It Out

Now we get to try it out. The following is a section of scripture for you here from Matthew's gospel and is entitled "The Wise & Foolish Builders." It's about six verses long and has some great content in it.

Everyone then who hears these words of mine and does them will be like a wise man who built his house on the¡ rock. And the rain fell, and the floods came, and the winds blew and beat on that house, but it did not fall, because it had been founded on the rock. And everyone who hears these words of mine and does not do them will be like a foolish man who built his house on the sand. And the rain fell, and the floods came, and the winds blew and beat against that house, and it fell, and great was the fall of it.

And when Jesus finished these sayings, the crowds were astonished at his teaching, for he was teaching them as one who had authority, and not as their scribes.
Matthew 7:24-29

So now, I want you to take a few minutes trying the Inductive Bible Study Method on your own. Take your time and see what you discover.

Your Inductive Bible Study Notes
- Observations
- Interpretation
- Application

What I Found in the Text

While I could walk you through many **observations** in this text, I am going to assume that you found most, if not all, of them. There were several things to observe. I'm also going to assume that in your **interpretation,** you uncovered that this is a short parable that appears at the close of the greatest sermon ever preached; the Sermon on the Mount. This sermon was preached by none other than Jesus Christ and written down later by Matthew, who wrote it as a witness to Jesus' life. Knowing this helps us to make the application that Matthew, and the preacher in Matthew, Jesus, wants us to hear.

But, the question we all want the answer to is, "What does this text mean to me?"

You could probably draw several of applications from this text, but there is one that Jesus does not want us to miss. That is: God's man needs to both **hear** and **do** in response to God's truth.

I believe this is one of the many challenges that Christian men face. Do we prefer to hear the truth and do nothing, or do we hear the truth and do something? Notice the problem is not a problem with the truth or hearing the truth, but a problem with integrating our hearing with our doing. This is what Jesus calls being "founded on the rock."

Consider this: have you ever attended church and find yourself being spiritually convicted by a sin, a struggle, an issue, or a problem, and then do nothing about it? If you answered "yes," then you have been guilty of "building your house on the sand." This is hearing and doing nothing. We've all done this (including me).

Jesus illustrates beautifully using a construction metaphor, the stark contrast between a man who only hears and a man who hears and acts, a the fully integrated man. Jesus makes it clear that everyone hears. The difference is the man who acts.

Jesus accentuates this by adding in a storm, a storm that exposes how well a man has integrated his hearing with his doing. Believe me, there will be a storm in your life at some point. This storm, regardless of how good the man looks on the exterior, will reveal the man of God on the interior, because every man experiences a storm. Either you're going into one, you're currently in one, or you're coming out of one. But the storm is eminent, fellas. So, the call to action by Jesus is to be prepared for the storm by integrating all of your life with his Word—both your hearing and doing—and thus build on the foundation, and the on the right foundation.

Well, gentlemen, I think you have your application for the week in this single question.

Have you integrated the hearing of God's Word with doing God's Word, so when the storms of life expose you for who you are at the core, you will stand firm?

Reflection & Discussion Questions:

- What part of the Inductive Bible Study Method was the most challenging?
- Based on the teaching of Matthew 7:24-29:
  - What action do you need to take?
  - What issues do you need to address?
  - Who is someone you could turn to for advice?

Call to Action

- Memorize the Inductive Bible Study Method.
- Try the Inductive Method on the first five sections of Matthew 7 this week. (verses Matthew 7:1-6, 7-11, 12-14, 15-20, and 21-23)
- Each day find a single application that will integrate your hearing and doing. Write it down on a sticky note and act on the application all day.

FUNDAMENTAL

2

SPIRITUAL RECEPTIVITY

I hope that over the last week you attempted some Inductive Bible Study on your own. If you did not get some reps in, we're going to do some today.

Before we dive in today, how about a little memory from my past?

When I was a teen, I took golf lessons at the prompting of my grandfather. As long as I have lived, I've valued those lessons. I remember my grandfather taking me to the club and watching me at practice. The pro would have me pull out a couple of clubs watch me swing and then correct my swing. At the end of each session, he would give me a 3" by 5" index card with a list of tips on them for each club I used that day. I had a stack of them that I kept with me for about a decade. When I was younger, these tips and tricks made me a better golfer.

But over the years, I have developed some terrible swinging habits and due to a lack of playing and practice. I may not have enough money to unlearn all the bad habits I have developed over the last 30 years; it may cost me an endless amount of money to relearn how to swing correctly again. So true, right?

When we launch into our spiritual journey we are so excited, but we also come with several misunderstandings about our faith. This is okay, because it takes a lifetime of unlearning to undo thoughts, attitudes, and actions we have done or developed in our natural life. One of those misunderstandings or misconceptions has to do with our spiritual development.

I think that many men believe that spiritual maturity is about either how much you spiritually know or about how spiritually old you are. But what if I told you your spiritual maturity has nothing to do with these two things? Nothing to do with how much you spiritually know or how spiritually old you are. You might think, thank God! But then you should immediately ask, what *is* it about? This is a great question, which we will answer today.

Pray

God, today help us to hear from you and act. Lead us, direct us, and teach us your secrets. In Christ's name—Amen.

Opener Reflection Questions

- We all pick up bad habits and patterns in our life. Where do we learn them? And why do we choose them?
- Is there a behavior you would like to unlearn today?
- What needs to happen for you to unlearn that behavior?

Jesus & His Secret to Maturity

In our text today, Jesus is going to give us the secret to spiritual maturity and the key to spiritual growth so that we can be increasingly productive in our spiritual lives. That's the goal and outcome of today's lesson.

To discover this secret, let's look at a text entitled the *Parable of the Sower*, found in Luke 8:4-15.

And when a great crowd was gathering and people from town after town came to him, he said in a parable, "A sower went out to sow his seed. And as he sowed, some fell along the path and was trampled underfoot, and the birds of the air devoured it. And some fell on the rock, and as it grew up, it withered away, because it had no moisture.

And some fell among thorns, and the thorns grew up with it and choked it. And some fell into good soil and grew and yielded a hundredfold." As he said these things, he called out, "He who has ears to hear, let him hear."

And when his disciples asked him what this parable meant, he said, "To you it has been given to know the secrets of the kingdom of God, but for others they are in parables, so that 'seeing they may not see, and hearing they may not understand.' Now the parable is this: The seed is the word of God.

The ones along the path are those who have heard; then the devil comes and takes away the word from their hearts, so that they may not believe and be saved. And the ones on the rock are those who, when they hear the word, receive it with joy. But these have no root; they believe for a while, and in time of testing fall away.

And as for what fell among the thorns, they are those who hear, but as they go on their way they are choked by the cares and riches and pleasures of life, and their fruit does not mature. As for that in the good soil, they are those who, hearing the word, hold it fast in an honest and good heart, and bear fruit with patience.

Luke 8:4-14

Study on Your Own

Now we are going to use our method from the last session. Remember: Inductive Bible Study begins with **Observations**, or what the text says. Then it moves into **Interpretation**, what the text meant to them. Then, finally comes the **Application,** what the text means to me.

The helpful acronym is O. I. A.

Try it on your own. Here is what I want you to do. First, **Re-read the Text**. Do this on your own and a few times. Remember, you can underline or circle keywords, grammar, make notes about the mood—or make any other notation you like. Second, walk through each one of the **Inductive Bible Study** steps, and then draw a single application.

My Notes (Observations, Interpretation, Application)

The Parable of the Sower

I bet you found all kinds of great things in this text!

I think this text is fun to study simply because of the **genre**. I want to make a special note of this here because the genre here is important. It's a *parable*. Parables are made up stories Jesus told to make a single spiritual application. They have this multi-dimensional feel because, as we read the text, we see real-life characters, like those speaking or listening to the story, but there are also characters *in* the story itself. Sometimes readers will end up allegorizing parables, which simply means we import representative symbols into the text. This is something want to avoid at all cost, unless of course, the teacher, in this case, Jesus, tells us in the text that those symbols mean something. So be careful when studying parables, don't import your ideas, symbols, or even your culture into the text (which is easy to do).

Let me share some of my observations, interpretation, and application, and we will see if mine match yours:

Observations

First, let's start with a few small observations. I notice several general things. A large crowd. A public and private teaching. A short portion of text from the Old Testament. There several other items, but if I had to pick three critical observations, they would be these: first there are four types of soil. They are hard, rocky, thorny, and good. Second, there are four types of results. They are nothing, sprouts and dies, sprout and grows but is chocked off, and produces incredible results. Third, the phrase that he calls out, "He who has ears to hear let him hear." I am sure you made these observations. They are connected and critical.

Interpretation

Now, as we interpret, we should ask the question, "What does this text mean to them?"

I believe the writer, who is Luke, wants us to know three things. First, he is telling us that Jesus is speaking in code to conceal his identity. At this time, he is only revealing it to a small inner circle of men. And second, he is also showing us how to decode the parables and teaching of Jesus, which is to give us this inside look at what happened early in Christ's ministry. If you continue to read Luke you will discover that Jesus slowly begins to reveal his mission and purpose. Third, he is giving us the secret, Jesus even calls it this, to spiritual success and productiveness. Also, he uses this farming image, something that everyone in an agrarian society *should* have understood—but as we see, they didn't.

Application

So what is the application?

Remember, in the application, we get to ask the question everyone asks to quickly, "What does this mean to me?" In this case, the application is relatively simple because Jesus gives us the application. He is teaching us that there are four levels of spiritual receptivity to God's truth.

- **Hard Soil**: The non-receptive heart, a person whose heart is unreceptive and rejects truth.
- **Rocky Soil**: The emotionally-receptive heart, a person whose heart is initially receptive but abandons truth when it encounters conflict or challenge.
- **Thorny Soil**: The conflict-adverse heart, a person whose heart is initially receptive but encounters too many other competing truths and then falls away.
- **Good Soil**: The receptive heart, a person who hears the truth, retains truth, and perseveres with the truth, and produces more truth.

From this, we discover all kinds of applications. Still, the one thing we learn more than anything else is the secret to spiritual maturity and key to spiritual success, and it's this: our spiritual receptivity! Jesus is concerned about my heart's receptivity more than anything else. Not how much I know, not how old I am, but if willing I am to listen, receive, and respond to his truth through the challenges of life.

And while we are quick in this text to classify other people and myself into one of these four categories, we need to be careful. I think we can exhibit all four soils, or have all four levels of receptivity at the same time. It just depends on the issue. For example, I can be very receptive to God's truth on the institution of marriage while being unreceptive to God's truth on divorce. Or I can be very receptive to God's truth on love until someone hates me, then become very unreceptive to turning the other cheek. You get the point: we all have varying levels of receptivity to truth, and we spend a lifetime tilling the soil of heart as we continue reading and discovering the truth one step at a time.

But *hear this* (and note the pun there): the defining factor of our spiritual maturity is not:

- How much we attend church.
- How much we give, serve, or volunteer.
- How much you know about the Bible.
- How many spiritual years you have put in.

The defining factor of our spiritual lives and spiritual growth is the receptivity of our hearts to God. This man produces results. Incredible results! Unthinkable results. It often astounds the people around him. Yes, you know men just like this. They have results but they are not aiming for the results. They are not seeking to magnify the results. They are aiming to be more receptive to God's truth, and he produces results through them.

But never forget the man with a receptive heart gives, serves, volunteers, and attends church with a purpose and pure motive. He does all these things, but does them for the right reason and with his focus on the right person. He is receptive to the change that needs to happen in him.

How about that for application.

So now the ball is in your court. What does this mean to you? You have to make this teaching personal. You cannot merely be inspired today. You are a man called to act.

Here is what I would do with a study like this. I would identify an area of my life where I have been unreceptive to change. Just one spot, not many. To determine this, think of a place where you have been resistant to change, and then ask yourself why? Take a moment to reflect on it, and then flip open the bible and find a verse that speaks to this topic. Then spend the week becoming more receptive to that one biblical truth in that one area. Don't try to do more. You cannot do it all. Take that one action: do it, do it daily, and take it deeper. It could be as simple as speaking kindly, removing harsh language, or patience with people, and then act on it daily.

Reflection & Discussion Questions:

- Where is a place in your life you are unreceptive to truth or change?
- Find a verse in the Bible that speaks to this topic.
- What issue do you need to address to become more receptive to this truth?
- What action can you take daily in response to the questions above?

Call to Action

- Post the verse you choose above in the comment section.
- Write your verse on a sticky note or in your journal and read it daily for seven days.
- Become receptive to the truth you need to hear, and then act on it daily for the next week.

FUNDAMENTAL

3

OVERVIEW OF THE BIBLE

Overwhelmed by the Bible

I am excited about today, as we are going to take a look at the Bible from a 30,000-foot view. The Bible is the most printed and most sold book of all time. I love this book, and even more the God who gave us this book. But I know we men often will look at this and become overwhelmed by its size and scope.

It's the same way we feel when we open a box from IKEA. You know that moment you rip open that box to discover 2,000 pieces to a cabinet that includes assembly instructions only an engineer could understand. Yep, you know what I am talking about. And here is the worst part, you are super-excited about what you bought, right? You just did not realize it was going to take three days to put together. So what ends up happening is your excitement quickly becomes discouragement because of the learning delay between purchase and use.

I think this is what it feels like for men when they become a Christian. They get a Bible and then open it for the first time, only to be confronted with discouragement because of its unique history, uncanny stories, and unusual characters. Because it looks too difficult to "put together," it sits on the shelf unused.

But today, I am hoping to help us overcome all this by giving you an overview with some tools that will aid you on your journey of reading God's Word. I want you to know if you are overwhelmed—it's normal. It took me years to discover the best tools that I am going to share with you today. But I believe they will aid you in reading and understanding the Word of God.

Goal

My goal today is to equip you with five tools that will help you enrichen your understanding of God's Word. Since there is a lot to discuss, I want to give you a brief outline:

First, we are going to take a look at the **Structure** of the whole Bible.

Second, we will overview the best **Study Helps** that will enrichen your reading and study.

Third, we will discover the various **Translations** of the Bible and why they are different.

Fourth, I will share a few **Important Facts** about the Bible.

Fifth, and finally, we will overview on **How the Bible Came Together** and became this collection we hold in our hands today.

But before we dig in, let's pray.

Pray
God, thanks for giving us your Word both spoken and in the flesh in Jesus Christ. I pray today that coming out of this time, we will have a fresh passion for your scripture, knowing that you have handed a timeless book that has had an eternal impact on the lives of men since time began. In your name—Amen.

Opener Reflection Questions
- What overwhelms you about the Bible?
- How often do you currently read the Bible?
- Would you like to read more? What's your motivation for wanting to read more?

Structure
Let's begin with the structure of the Bible. Years ago Mortimer Adler taught us that there is a way to read a book, and it all starts with understanding the general outline of the book itself.

So, in an attempt to get a handle on this book, it is good to know that the Bible contains 66 individual books divided into two Covenants (or "Testaments"), one old and one new. (And keep in mind the word "old" does not mean it's no longer valid.)

This book tells one story. It's the Story of God and his son, Jesus Christ.

Now the two testaments are organized into sections.

In the Old Testament, you have five sections:

- LAW
- HISTORY
- POETRY
- MAJOR PROPHETS
- MINOR PROPHETS

In the New Testament, you have six sections:
- GOSPELS
- HISTORY
- PAUL'S LETTERS
- HEBREWS
- LETTERS TO CHURCHES
- PROPHECY

Breakdown of the themes of each book

THE OLD TESTAMENT

LAW
Genesis: The Election of God.
Exodus: The Redemption of God.
Leviticus: The Holiness of God.
Numbers: The Faithfulness of God.
Deuteronomy: Obedience to God.

HISTORY
Joshua: Possession of the Land.
Judges: The Book of Apostasy.
Ruth: Redemption by a Kinsman.

1 Samuel: Establishment of the Kingdom.
2 Samuel: Expansion of the Kingdom.
1 Kings: Division of the Kingdom.
2 Kings: Destruction of the Kingdom.
1 Chronicles: Preparing for the Temple.
2 Chronicles: Building of the Temple.
Ezra: The Book of Restoration.
Nehemiah: The Book of Continual Restoration.
Ester: The Providence of God.

POETRY

Job: Suffering of the Righteous.
Psalms: The Book of Praise.
Proverbs: The Book of Wisdom.
Ecclesiastes: The Book of the Futility of Life.
Song of Solomon: The Book of Love.

MAJOR PROPHETS

Isaiah: The Salvation of God.
Jeremiah: The Judgment of God.
Lamentations: The Lament.
Ezekiel: The Glory of God.
Daniel: The Sovereignty of God.

MINOR PROPHETS

Hosea: The Love of God.
Joel: The Day of the Lord.
Amos: The Judgment of God.
Obadiah: Judgment on Edom.
Jonah: The Grace of God.
Micah: Summons to Judgment.
Nahum: Judgment on Nineveh.
Habakkuk: The Righteousness of God.
Zephaniah: The Day of the Lord.
Haggai: Rebuilding the Temple.

Zechariah: The Future of Jerusalem.
Malachi: The Charges of God.

THE NEW TESTAMENT

GOSPELS
Matthew: The Kingship of Jesus Christ.
Mark: The Servanthood of Jesus Christ.
Luke: The Humanity of Jesus Christ.
John: The Deity of Jesus Christ.

HISTORY
Acts: The Spread of Christianity.

PAUL'S LETTERS
Romans: The Righteousness of God.
1 Corinthians: Disorders in the Church.
2 Corinthians: True Ministry.
Galatians: Freedom from the Mosaic Law.
Ephesians: Calling of the Believer.
Philippians: Living Worthy of the Gospel.
Colossians: The Sufficiency of Christ.
1 Thessalonians: The Book of Sanctification.
2 Thessalonians: The Book of the Correction of Prophecy.
1 Timothy: Conduct of the Church.
2 Timothy: Ministry of the Word.
Titus: Order in the Church.
Philemon: Example of Love.

LETTER TO HEBREW DISCIPLES
Hebrews: The Superiority of Christ

LETTERS TO CHURCHES
James: Handling Trials.
1 Peter: Salvation of the Soul.
2 Peter: The Second Coming of Christ.
1 John: Fellowship with the True God.

2 John: The Truth of God.
3 John: The Practice of Love.
Jude: The Book of False Teachers.

PROPHECY
Revelation: Judgment by Jesus Christ.

I believe knowing this gives you a solid 30,000-foot view of the Bible. When I begin reading a single book from among this library of books, I consider where the book is in the Bible, and the type of genre and book theme. This is helpful because when I acknowledge the macro-narrative, then the micro-narrative beings to make more sense, which helps me to understand the text correctly.

Study Helps
So, next, let's take a look at some great study helps.

I want to walk you through several resources that can complement any Bible Study. I organize these tools into six categories. But keep in mind that there are hundreds, if not thousands, of these on the market today. This is the reason why I am giving you an overview. Often there are so many that a reader doesn't know where to begin.

As I work down my list, you will note I am listing them by the degree to which I find them helpful for the average reader.

First, we have the **Commentary:**

Commentaries are books written by theologians that explain a book of the bible. So they take one book and explain things like authorship, history, setting, and theme or themes. They often "comment" verse-by-verse. Now you can buy them individually. For example, you can get one for the book of Genesis or Matthew. But if you were to get one, I think the Study Bible is the best version of a commentary for beginners, because you get the Bible and the commentary built-in.

Second, we have the **Lexicon:**

Lexicons provide definitions and meanings of biblical words found in the original languages. (I will discuss the languages of the Bible a little later.) Some students of the Bible, who love language and word studies, usually have one of these.

Third, we have the **Concordance:**

These are used for finding words and meanings in the original languages and offer deeper understandings of terms and where they are found throughout the Bible.

Fourth, we have the **Dictionary:**

You probably don't need a lot of explanation here, but these are helpful tools. But this is a *Bible* dictionary, not a popular dictionary like the one Webster puts out. They usually combine definitions with verse references that help readers to define and analyze texts.

Fifth, we have the **Encyclopedia:**

Remember, this is a *Bible* Encyclopedia. These contain articles and definitions of words and terms used in Scripture. Entries usually include full historical references such as dates, religious environment, family life, customs, language, and literature.

Sixth, we have what is called the **Apocryphal Books:**

I have included this one since these texts are books included as part of the Septuagint (which is the Greek version of the Old Testament). The Roman Catholic and Orthodox Bibles have all of the Apocrypha (except the books of Esdras and the Prayer of Manasseh) but refer to them as "deuterocanonical" books in the Catholic church. Protestant Bibles do not include the Apocrypha. If you are curious about what's in them, they can all be found online for your reading pleasure. I will address why they are not in the Bible I hold in my hand.

So, this is a brief overview.

For the most part, you do not need to buy any of these. There are plenty of online resources available today and for free—unless you want a Study Bible.

Translations

Next, let's take a look at the various translations of the Bible. Yes, the Bible is a book that is translated into the English language. The Old Testament was written in Hebrew and the New Testament in Greek. Therefore, since most of us don't read or speak ancient Hebrew or Greek, we need to have someone translate it.

When people look to purchase a bible today, most are shocked by the overwhelming numbers of translations of the Bible. We really shouldn't be surprised by it. Two factors play into this. First, when culture changes, so does the language. For example, who would have ever thought "selfie" would become a word? But when culture makes a shift like this, the language adapts, and thus our translation must evolve. This is why we have so many English variations. Second, there are various methodologies used to translate the ancient text. I am going to walk you through the three main methods, and I think this will be super helpful for you in understanding the types of Bibles we have on the market today. They are: *Word for Word*, *Thought for Thought*, and *Paraphrase*.

First, you have the **Word for Word** approach. The technical name for this approach is the "Formal Equivalent," and it is a method that translates the Bible one word at a time. There are a few translations that use this approach. You've probably seen their acronyms before. Versions like the NASB, which stands for the *New American Standard Bible*, the ESV, which stands for the *English Standard Version*, and the RSV, which stands for the *Revised Standard Version*.

There are particular strengths to using this approach, such as greater reliance on the original text, less interpretation by the translator. It's suitable for in-depth word study, and more precision in translation. But there are also weaknesses. This means a Word for Word translation can read awkwardly at times, require more effort to interpret, be difficult for young people or new Christians to read, and result in readers reaching the wrong conclusions, which will impact their application.

Second, you have the **Thought for Thought** approach. The technical name for this approach is the "Functional Equivalent," and this is a method that translates the Bible, usually considering a sentence at a time. There are a few translations of the Bible that use this approach. They are the NIV, which stands for the New International Version, or the NLT, which stands for the New Living Translation.

The strengths of this approach are it is easier to read, it conveys meaning, it's great for public reading, and trained scholars interpret the text for you. The weaknesses would be it requires less study, it's not as beneficial for word study, and often reads in longer sentences because of the need to explain a technical term using a phrase.

Third, you have the **Paraphrase,** which is simply that: it paraphrases large paragraphs at one time. While it is poetic, it's not helpful for study, and I would not recommend purchasing a paraphrase. Even though I do have a couple of copies on my shelf, I'll let you know I never use them. An example of one would be *The Message*, a Bible written by Eugene Peterson.

So, there you have it, three approaches to translating the Bible, which leads us to numerous versions. Here is a text sampling of Genesis 28:14 that will illustrate the comparison between the versions we just discussed.

NASB – In you and in your descendants shall all the families of the earth be blessed.
ESV - In you and your offspring shall all the families of the earth be blessed.
RSV - By you and your descendants shall all the families of the earth bless themselves.
KJV - In thee and in thy seed shall all the families of the earth be blessed.
NKJV - In you and in your seed all the families of the earth shall be blessed.
NRSV - All the families of the earth shall be blessed in you and in your offspring.
NIV - All peoples on earth will be blessed through you and your offspring.
CEV - Your family will be a blessing to all people.
MSG - All the families of the Earth will bless themselves in you and your descendants.
LB - And all the nations of the earth will be blessed through you and your descendants.

A List of Facts about the Bible

God inspired more than 40 individuals to write the Bible over nearly 2,000 years.

The word "Bible" is derived from the Greek word "biblia," meaning "book." The term "biblia" gets its roots from the word "byblos," meaning papyrus. Papyrus was the material used for text at that time. The ancient Greeks obtained their supplies of paper (papyrus) from the port of Byblos, located in modern-day Lebanon.

The Old Testament contains 39 books; the New Testament contains 27. In total, the Bible includes 66 divinely inspired books. These books are motivated by God, not the men who wrote them. These men were are fallible and fallen just like you and me, yet God used them for his purposes. Two significant contributors were Moses, who wrote the first five books of the Old Testament, and Paul, who wrote 14 books of the New Testament.

The Bible includes two testaments known as the Old and New Testament. The word "testament" means "will," "covenant," or "agreement." The Old Testament contains and demonstrates God's promise. The New Testament His fulfillment of the covenant of grace and salvation. These two testaments form the complete book known as the Christian Holy Bible.

The terms "Old Testament" and "New Testament" originated with the prophet Jeremiah. When Jeremiah referenced Israel's future, he proclaimed God would "*make a new covenant with the house of Israel.*" Jesus of Nazareth, the long-awaited Messiah, made that new covenant with God's people. The books of the New Testament provide the fulfillment of the promises made throughout the Old Testament.

The Old Testament was originally written in the Hebrew language, with a few verses or portions of Jeremiah, Daniel, and Ezra written in Aramaic (a dialect developed during the Jewish captivity that gradually took the place of Hebrew as the common language of the Jewish people). The New Testament was originally written in Greek.

The Jewish Bible is the equivalent of our Old Testament.

Under Ptolemy rule, the Hebrew Scriptures were translated into the *Koine* Greek dialect. The translation, an outstanding literary accomplishment, is called the Septuagint. Ptolemy II Philadelphus sponsored the translation project around the third century B.C. According to tradition, 72 Jewish scholars (six from each of the twelve tribes) were summoned for the project, and the work was completed in 72 days.

Most Jews of Jesus' day spoke Aramaic, a commonly spoken Syrian language similar to Hebrew. It is not known if Jesus spoke Greek as he left no personal writings.

No doubt, Jesus studied the formal Hebrew of the Torah, Prophets, and Writings (Old Testament) because Jewish boys diligently studied these texts. By the age of 12, Jesus would have been able to recite them by heart. He would have learned by rote from scrolls kept by local teachers or rabbis.

There are more than 24,000 partial and complete manuscript copies of the New Testament. These ancient manuscript copies are public.

How the Bible Came Together?

One of the most popular questions people like me get about the Bible is how did it come together as a book? This is a great question. If this book is 66 individual books, how did these books come together?

There is a technical word for this: *canon*. Not cannon, like the big gun that is spelled a little different. Canon is a word that means *"criteria by which something is judged."* Think of this word like you would a ruler or measuring stick. So, when we discuss the Canonization of the Bible, we are talking about the process of decision making by which these 66 books ended up together, and thus their validity.

Now in your handbook I reference I am not going to read through all the dates on the timeline, you can do that on your own, but I am going to touch on three critical dates.

First, note the date: 140 A.D. Everything begins with controversy, right? So Marcion is the person who launched us into our need for Bible canonization because, as a result of his incorrect interpretation of the God of the OT and NT, a bunch of theologians came together to discuss what of the books should be considered biblical canon. Remember, Marcion is not questioning the authorship of the books or their validity because this was widely accepted. What he was questioning was theological interpretation. But this stirred the need to address other bigger issues.

Second, by the date 367 A.D., we have the bible as we hold in our hands today. So that means for the last approximately 1,600 years, we have the text as it would have been read in the fourth century. Christians by this time have gathered the text, and most astounding, we discover that the debate was not about the validity of the Bible but rather just a few small details regarding the New Testament books and gathering full agreement about these smaller details.

Third, you are going to notice on the timeline that there were several dates that church Councils argued over these details. Councils were formal gatherings where great Christian thinkers came together to discuss all these issues. You will notice this happened over many years. What you should see here is that they took this very seriously, and what resulted was the book we hold in our hands today.

50-100 A.D.: Writing of the New Testament.

140 A.D.: Marcion, an influential businessman in Rome, taught the heresy of two gods: "Yahweh," the cruel god of the Old Testament, and "Abba," the kind father of the New Testament. Marcion eliminated the Old Testament scriptures, and since he was anti-Semitic, he kept only ten letters of Paul and 2/3 of Luke's gospel (he deleted references to Jesus' Jewishness). Marcion's false New Testament, the first to be compiled, forced the Church to

decide on a core canon. That original canon included the four Gospels and Letters of Paul.

200 A.D.: The periphery of the canon is not yet determined. According to one list compiled in Rome (The Muratorian Canon), the New Testament consisted of the four gospels, Acts, 13 letters of Paul, three of the seven General Epistles (1 John, 2 John, and Jude); and what's known as the Apocalypse of Peter.

367 A.D.: The earliest extant list of the books of the New Testament, in exactly the number and order we have today, is written by St. Athanasius, Bishop of Alexandria.

382 A.D.: Council of Rome meets where Pope Damasus starts the process of defining a universal canon for the Church. The New Testament books are listed in their present number and order.

393 A.D.: At the Council of Hippo, leaders argue, St. Athanasius proposes his Canon.

397 A.D.: The Council of Carthage refines the Canon, sending it to Pope Innocent for ratification. In the East, the canonical process is hampered by several schisms (especially within the Church of Antioch).

787 A.D.: The Ecumenical Council of Nicaea II adopts the Canon of Carthage. At this point, both the Latin West and the Greek-Byzantine East hold the same canon. However, the non-Greek Monophysite and Nestorian Churches of the East (the Copts, the Ethiopians, the Syrians, the Armenians, the Syro-Malankars, the Chaldeans, and the Malabars) still didn't agree. These Churches joined in agreement, in 1442 A.D. in Florence.

1227 A.D.: Bible divided into chapters by Stephen Langton, Archbishop of Canterbury. The chapters were divided into verses at a later date.

1442 A.D.: At the Council of Florence, the entire Church recognized the 27 books. This council confirmed the Roman Catholic Canon of the Bible, which Pope Damasus I had published a thousand years earlier. By 1439, 100 years before the Reformation, all orthodox branches of the Church were legally bound to the same canon.

1536 A.D.: In his translation of the Bible from Greek into German, Luther removed four New Testament books (Hebrews, James, Jude, and Revelation) and placed them in an appendix.

1546 A.D.: At the Council of Trent, the Catholic Church reaffirmed once and for all the complete canon. The council also confirmed the inclusion of the deuterocanonical books, which had been a part of the biblical canon since the early Church and was confirmed at the councils of 393 AD, 373, 787, and 1442 AD.

1550 A.D.: Bible divided into verses by Robert Estienne (a.k.a. Robert Stephens), a Parisian printer.

I want you to know there is so much more we could discuss on this topic, but this gives you a solid overview of five bits of information that will strengthen your trust in this book and the God who inspired it.

I want to encourage you before next week to make sure you bring a Bible with you each week. Get one you enjoy, that you are willing to carry with you. I know we can also use a Bible on our devices, but I think it's beneficial to have something with us that we can get used to, carry with us, take notes in, and reference for a long time in our spiritual lives.

Men will often ask me which version I use. My preference is the ESV or the English Standard Version. I choose this version because I prefer to study the Bible on my own, which is what we do here. If I could make a recommendation to you, I would say get the combo Bible and Commentary, which is called the *ESV Study Bible*. That way, the commentary is built in. But I will warn you it is a little more expensive.

But remember the best thing we can do is not *buy* a Bible, it's *getting into it*—frequently.

Reflection & Discussion Questions:
- Which of the five tools that we discussed did you find most interesting?
- How did or does this help you in your faith?

Call to Action
- Get a Bible if you do not have one.
- Share which bible you have or will be using.
- Flip through your bible this week. Get familiar with it.

FUNDAMENTAL

4

THE PROFIT OF SCRIPTURE

We Need the Right Direction

When I was younger, I used to work on cars all the time. Back in the day we used to have these manuals we would go to for information on how to fix a car; they were called Chilton manuals. These were incredible for properly repairing any automobile. And every car had a manual for that respective year, make, and model.

Today, occasionally, I still tinker on cars, but remember, I also have a lot of other responsibilities that keep from this hobby. But a few years back, someone gave, outright *gave* me, a car that I was excited to work and restore. It was a 1958 VW Beetle. Now I have owned several classic cars in my lifetime, but the Beetle was one of my favorites because it is so easy to work on.

Today, when I work on a car, do you know where I go? Not Chilton manual, I go to YouTube, because I can find experts who show you exactly what to do step by step visually. I cannot tell you how many times I have been to YouTube to fix items on many of my cars. The visual, audio and educational format is much better than the old Chilton manuals. When you find someone who knows what they are doing with that make and model of car, it's super helpful to get all the information you need.

I think that principle applies to the topic today. When it comes to the issues we face in life as men, the person best to go to is our Creator. The designer of man himself—God—and his instruction book on how we should live: the Bible. But you know this is not where we always go for advice on how to live. And you know this is true.

Goal

So my goal today's lesson is to help you see the importance and payoff of scripture so that you will turn to God and his Word more frequently for the direction you need as a man of God.

Before we begin, let's pray.

Pray

God, thanks for creating us, all mankind, and me. Thank you for not only creating me but being the Creator and giving me direction for how to best live life each day. Help me today to trust more in you and your plan for my life. In Christ's name—Amen.

Opener Reflection Questions

- When you are angry, depressed, frustrated, or anxious, where do you turn for answers? Be honest, what's your first impulse, and where do you go or what do you do?
- Identify and briefly describe the biggest life issue that you struggle with at this time. What are your thoughts about that issue?
- In the past, how have you tried to overcome this problem? Have your efforts worked?
- How do you think God views the situation?

It's Profitable

I want to briefly look at a scripture that has a lot to say about this topic. The apostle Paul, a New Testament author, is writing a letter to his protégé, Timothy. In doing so, he is giving him some critical advice on God's Word. Here is what he says to him.

> *All Scripture is breathed out by God and profitable for teaching, for reproof, for correction, and for training in righteousness, that the man of God may be complete, equipped for every good work.*
> **2 Timothy 3:16-17**

I love this instruction and these verses because they give not only Timothy needed direction, but us today some critical information that we need to cling to as followers of Jesus Christ.

So let's look at two very descriptive words here. Notice these are observations. First, notice the word "breathed." This is a choice word by Paul. It's very descriptive. In Paul's words to Timothy, we learn that God is "breathing" out scripture. That scripture comes deliberately, naturally, and actively from God. His breath is like oxygen for our existence, thus we can conclude that scripture is the imperative oxygen of our spiritual life, and without it, we do not have life. This is not the only time this image appears in the Bible. If you turn back to the beginning of the Bible, Genesis 2, we see similar imagery. Here is how it reads.

> Then the Lord God formed the man of dust from the ground and breathed into his nostrils the breath of life, and the man became a living creature.
> **Genesis 2:7**

This just punctuates what I think Paul is saying here. That our same Creator, who breathed physical life into us from that very first breath, is also the one who sustains us daily through the breath of his word, his scripture is our spiritual oxygen that provides fuel for our existence.

But there is another keyword and observation here. It's the word "profit." This again is a word with a lot of imagery, but this tells us why scripture's essential. Scripture is important because it has a profit—which is to have an advantage or gain.

Now fellas, there a lot of things in life that do not have a guaranteed profit. Like my retirement account, social security, or perhaps your business, and on some days, your sales cycle. But guess what Scripture has profit every single time. Yes, every single time. It is profitable. It is the only thing in this life that is guaranteed to have a profit every single time. And this is awesome, because who does not want to have a guarantee on investment. A 100% money-back guarantee.

With these two key observations, Paul has set us up to see four God-breathed guaranteed profits.

Profit 1: Teaching. Scripture is profitable for **showing** us the path.

Profit 2: Reproof. Scripture is profitable for showing us **when we stray off** the path.

Profit 3: Correction. Scripture is profitable for showing us **how to get back on** the path.

Profit 4: Training. Scripture is profitable for showing us **how to stay on** the path.

These are four ways we profit from scripture every single time; and if you have been a follower of Christ even for a short period, you will discover the power and profit of scripture.

An Example of Profit

When I was about 16 years old, I remember being desperate for direction in my life. One day, attending a church with my grandparents, I remember the teaching pastor ending his sermon with this challenge. He said, "If you read Colossians 3 every day for a month, it will change your life forever." Well, if you would have heard this from my perspective on this day in my life, you would have heard this statement a little different. How I heard it was, "If you read Colossians 3 every day for a month, God will show up and do something miraculous in your life."

So, I went home and stole my Grandmother's old Bible. I still have it today. (And no kidding: I read that chapter every single day.) Some days I read it a few times. As I got closer to day 30, my anticipation continued to build. With excitement came day 28, then 29, and then day 30. On day 30, I woke up early, and I read that chapter one last time. I closed the book and just waited, and waited, and waited, and guess what—nothing happened! In disappointment, I closed the book, and unfortunately for me, this became evidence that God was not real, and that pastor was a poser.

Fast-forward a couple of years into the future. I had moved out of my grandfather's home and was living out on my own and pursing life as I saw fit. I was making some poor decisions on who I was spending time with and engaging in behavior that were not very beneficial in my life. In a moment of clarity, one where I started to come to my senses, I realized that a lot of my decisions and relationships were destroying my life. I was not a good place financially, relationally, or ethically and now I found myself having the same conversation I had with God years ago. In this moment of despair, I remember asking God to make clear if he was real. And then it happened. Those words from Colossians 3 came rushing back at me. You see, those words I had read from the past were embedded into my memory. I had unintentionally memorized the whole chapter by merely reading that chapter daily for a month. The results of exposing myself to God's breath was working for my profit—I just did not realize it until later. God's Word ultimately led me back to him.

You see, I encountered the real profit of the word of God. Here is what God says about his word Isaiah 55:11.

> *"So shall my word be that goes out from my mouth; it shall not return to me empty, but it shall accomplish that which I purpose, and shall succeed in the thing for which I sent it."*
> **Isaiah 55:11**

The point is this; Scripture brings profit every single time you read it. Sometimes it is realized immediately. Other times it is recognized later. But the profit is realized and 100% guaranteed.

The Implications of Scripture

I want to draw your attention to that closing phrase by Paul in 2 Timothy 3:17. He says this.

> *All Scripture is breathed out by God and profitable for teaching, for reproof, for correction, and for training in righteousness,* ***that the man of God may be complete, equipped for every good work.***
> **2 Timothy 3:16-17**

The results of scripture and its profit is that we become complete and equipped, which is what we are all looking for in this life. Purpose. Fulfillment. Happiness. Paul knows that all men want this, including his protégé Timothy. But it is also important to clarify what this implies and does not imply so that we understand how this applies in our everyday life.

Here are five implications of the profit of scripture, which results in us being "complete, equipped for every good work."

First, "complete and equipped" implies that God's Word is **essential** for our direction as men. Gentlemen, Scripture is the only and essential guide for our life. There is no other self-help book, suggestion from a friend, or strategic method that will give you direction like God's Word. It is essential.

Second, "complete and equipped" does imply that God's Word is **everything** we need for life and godliness. If you want to develop godly character, you have to go to God to find out how to be godly.

Third, "complete and equipped" does imply that God's Word must be **read habitually**. This book is not an accessory. It's time to dust it off, break the binding, and start digging in.

Fourth, "complete and equipped" does not imply we **worship the Bible**. Worship of the bible has a designation; it is called bibliolatry, which is another form of idolatry. We have to remember scripture points us to God, and it's God whom we worship, not the Bible.

And fifth, "complete and equipped" does not imply that God's Word is **exhaustive**. Scripture does not address every situation of our life, but its principles address everything of consequence that we would need for life and godliness.

So, by the breath of God, we profit given these implications as men of God.

Reflection & Discussion Questions:
- Which of the two keywords, "breath" or "profit," captured your attention and why?
- How does understanding the four profits of scripture encourage you to turn to it more often?
- There were five implications of scripture. Which one most impacted you?

Call to Action

- Memorize 2 Timothy 3:16-17. Somehow find a method for committing this to memory this week.

FUNDAMENTAL
5

We've Missed the Mark

Today we are going to attempt to understand sin. For some of us, this is a topic we know way too much about. I know it is not a fun topic, but it is one of great importance. One of the great ways we learn is by making mistakes. Pain is often a man's predominant teacher. Listen to this quote from John Wooden. He said:

If you're not making mistakes, then you're not doing anything.
I'm positive that a doer makes mistakes.
John Wooden

But in this case, we are not simply talking about making a mistake. We are talking about *sin*.

Now, sin is a biblical word, which means "to miss the mark." If you follow Olympic competitions, you may remember a big story from the 2004 Olympic Games about a guy named Matthew Emmons. Emmons competed in the 50-meter three-position rifle competition for the U.S. As the favored contestant, he was set to take the Gold without much effort. All he needed to do was hit the final target anywhere in his last shot. So, he sets, aims, shoots, and nails the bullseye. But unfortunately, he struck the bullseye of the target in the next lane. Because of this error, he did not score, and dropped to eighth place. Of course, he became the leading illustration of what it means to miss the mark.

We are not talking about missing the mark in target shooting. We are talking about spiritually missing the mark, and therefore not hitting God's standard for righteous living. This is not to merely "make a mistake;" we are talking about an offense directed at God himself.

Goal

The goal in today's lesson is to discover the bait of sin, how we rationalize sin, and the results of sin so that we can understand and engage the battle with sin more effectively.

Pray

God, we know we are indeed sinful and that all mankind falls short of your righteousness. Help us today as a result of this time to have a clearer understanding of sin and how to engage the battle. In Christ's name—Amen.

Opener Reflection Questions

- What was a "dumb" mistake you made as a kid? How did this mistake affect you even into the future?
- What are some of the most prevalent issues men face today that God would call sins?
- What impact are these sins having on our culture or world?

The Bait of Sin

Today, we are going to read from a significant portion of Genesis 3. In this chapter, we get a clear glimpse of sin, if not one of the best understandings of sin in the whole Bible. This one chapter holds the secrets to why, how, and what happens when we sin and even what God does to come to our rescue. Note, if you are ever looking for an understanding of sin, just flip back to this chapter of the Bible.

Let's read the first few verses, and then we will take a look at what baits mankind into sin.

> Now the serpent was more crafty than any other beast of the field that the Lord God had made. He said to the woman, "Did God actually say, 'You shall not eat of any tree in the garden'?" And the woman said to the serpent, "We may eat of the fruit of the trees in the garden, but God said, 'You shall not eat of the fruit of the tree that is in the midst of the garden, neither shall you touch it, lest you die.'"

> *But the serpent said to the woman, "You will not surely die. For God knows that when you eat of it your eyes will be opened, and you will be like God, knowing good and evil."*
> ## Genesis 3:1-5

Here are three quick insights on how we fall for the bait of sin. I think the term *bait* is so appropriate here. Because the woman in this instance falls for this hook, line, and sinker. So here are the key texts and the subsequent baits.

Bait one is **Questioning the Truth**. Notice verse two. It reads, *"Did God actually say, 'You shall not eat of any tree in the garden'?"* So what's the serpent doing here? Well, he's trying to lure the woman into doubting the precision of the command so that she will question God himself. He's trying to get woman to examine not just the accuracy of the truth but the intent of the truth and therefore examine the character and trustworthiness of the one who gave it.

This is *always* the first bait. We question the limits and the boundaries of truth. If you have children, you know this is what children do. They question the truth and the trustworthiness of the parent who gave them that truth, especially if they see other peers doing something that they want to do. But this is not something only kids do; it's something we all do. And when we do so, we can be tempted to fall for this first bait, the bait of questioning the truth, and thus questioning God.

Bait two is **Twisting the Truth**. Notice verse four; it reads, *"You will not surely die."* At this moment, mankind (which was only Adam and Eve) had little if no understanding of death. Clearly, they had not personally experienced it. In the mystery of this moment, the serpent takes God's command and twists it ever so slightly. He presents the idea that death would not be a factor. He twists it just enough to eliminate the effects of sin in the woman's mind. Of course, we do discover after the incident, that the serpent was partially correct. That man and woman did not die—immediately. But eventually, they did both die—physically and spiritually. Physical death did result. Spiritual death, which we call separation from God, was another result. Both were tragic results, and we have been feeling the effects ever since this moment.

Gentlemen, this is one of the baits of sin. We all fall for time and time again: hook, line, and sinker. We, in our mind, hear a twist on the truth, and then fall for it because we see a slight advantage. Then we justify it and go after it fast so as not to miss out on the benefit—and then most of the time we are disappointed by the unintended results.

Bait three is the **Desire for More**. Verse five reads, *"For God knows that when you eat of it your eyes will be opened, and you will be like God, knowing good and evil."* Here the serpent convinces the woman that she needs something she doesn't currently have. But notice he has already warmed her up to this. When she took the first bait, she is questioning the truth, and now it's twisted, and then he throws out the tasty worm: you want more.

Notice what the desire is for: *"to be like God."* Now, this is a bold proposition, right? But this is the ultimate bait for all mankind. We want to be in control. We want to have power. We want to be the man. We want to be God. It's this insidious desire that lies at the core of all sin. This is the ultimate bait—but in taking the bait we become *less like God*, not more. While we don't often admit this as men, it's this desire that results in man's darkest moments and deepest issues.

These are the baits of sin. I believe if we spent a little time reflecting on our sin issues, we would find that it was these three baits that lure us into disobedience in relationship with God.

The Rationalization of Sin

But, let's not just talk about the bait of sin and what leads up to it. I also want to address what is happening in our minds right before this moment of sin. In this text, there is one verse that tells us what was going on in the mind of the woman right before she sinned. And the lesson is critical to us understanding how we think about sin, how we rationalize it, and how we might even stop the progression of sin.

So let's look at Genesis 3:6:

So when the woman saw that the tree was good for food, and that it was a delight to the eyes, and that the tree was to be desired to make one wise, she took of its fruit and ate, and she also gave some to her husband who was with her, and he ate.

Genesis 3:6

We rationalize sin more than we think we do. It happens quickly. But I am so glad this one verse appears in our Bible because it tells us just how we in our minds rationalize or justify at that moment right before we sin. And note this: the serpent understands that he cannot make her, or her husband sin, he can only lead them toward sin. It is the individual that must take the step. But we take the first step closer to a sin in our mind.

So here are three rationalizations we make.

Rationalization one, **<u>"It's good."</u>** This is where in our mind, we choose to relabel something that is bad, good. Did you catch that in verse six? She now looks at the tree and see's the fruit and perceives it in her mind to be good. Yes, it was always good, but it was wrong to eat. But now she is rationalizing toward herself so that she can gain an advantage.

This is always our first step in our minds. We start rationalizing toward ourselves. We think things like this:

- *"A little bit won't hurt."*
- *"No one will ever know."*
- *"It's doesn't matter if I do it one time."*
- *"I deserve it."*

If you have said any of these things in your mind, you have rationalized or justified your actions even before acting. You have done exactly what this woman did here.

Rationalization two, **<u>"It's a delight."</u>** Coming back to our verse, here is what happens in her mind. She saw *"that it was a delight to the eyes."* At this point, her mind is choosing only to see the pleasure that will come from making the decision. Some might call this confirmation bias. But what happens is she sees only the pleasure it will bring, and therefore is blinded to the negative outcomes.

Now we must recognize that there is always some benefit to sin. Sin does have some immediate delight. It has some delight; otherwise, we would never do it. It's the positive payoff, the pleasure, and the delight that we want, not the negative consequences. For example, we embezzle money because we want a little bit more without the effort. Or we commit adultery because we want power, sex, and intimacy that maybe we are not currently getting. Or we exaggerate the truth because we want to appear more successful or show someone up. But in this pursuit of pleasure, we don't often think that we will get fired if we embezzle money, or destroy our family if we commit adultery, or damage our character if we exaggerate the truth. This short-sighted pursuit of pleasure is the next step we take in our minds. We are just one step closer to sin.

Rationalization three, **"It's wisdom."** So notice that at this point her mind has played the trump card. Here is what the text says, *"and that the tree was to be desired to make one wise."* She now has connected the future results to what her mind has already rationalized. In the business world, we call this vision. Her picture of the future is so clear that she cannot help but act upon it.

But all that is missing is the action. That's what we see next. Notice the action words that follow this three-pronged rationalization. She *"she took,"* she *"ate,"* *"she also gave,"* and *"he ate."* Then sin, which was only a mental appetite, is birthed into physical action. James 1:15 says it this way:

> *Then desire when it has conceived gives birth to sin,*
> *and sin when it is fully grown brings forth death.*
> **James 1:15**

The rationalization here of the woman is not something exclusive to her. Please note, the man, that's our gender, participated as well. While we don't see what's happening in our mind in this text, we can see by his action that he wanted all of the same things; otherwise, he would have done something. Before woman was ever created, God gave man this command, and yet in the face of injustice and sin, man does nothing and says nothing. Notice in all of Genesis chapter 3 while all this is going on, we don't see a peep from man, God's greatest creation with whom he gave power, dominion, authority, and a single moral command regarding this tree and its fruit. And yet he, too, falls for the bait and rationalization of sin, which is clarified by his subsequent actions.

The Response to Sin
But there is still more. More bad news.

In the later part of Genesis 3, we will get to see how they respond to this whole situation after they actively disobey God. Here is how the text reads in Genesis 3:7-13

> *Then the eyes of both were opened, and they knew that they were naked. And they sewed fig leaves together and made themselves loincloths. And they heard the sound of the Lord God walking in the garden in the cool of the day, and the man and his wife hid themselves from the presence of the Lord God among the trees of the garden. But the Lord God called to the man and said to him, "Where are you?"*
>
> *And he said, "I heard the sound of you in the garden, and I was afraid, because I was naked, and I hid myself." He said, "Who told you that you were naked? Have you eaten of the tree of which I commanded you not to eat?" The man said, "The woman whom you gave to be with me, she gave me fruit of the tree, and I ate." Then the Lord God said to the woman, "What is this that you have done?" The woman said, "The serpent deceived me, and I ate."*
>
> **Genesis 3:7-13**

Now there are a ton of observations we can make here, and we could spend all day on this text. But I want you to notice these two responses.

First, the initial response is to **cover and hide**. This is their automatic first response. Notice that their *"eyes were opened,"* which means they now fully understand—they get it. The confirmation bias is gone. But this act of disobedience reveals new emotions and new responses, specifically guilt and shame, that results in concealing and hiding. They do what any person would do in sin, they cover by making loincloths, and they hide when God shows up on the scene.

Second, notice the second response is to **blame**. This is because shame usually leads to blame. But while we tend to blame others, notice who the man and woman are blaming. They are not blaming each other: they are blaming God. The man blames the woman who God created, and the woman blames the serpent who God also created. While God allows them to confess, even though he knows what they have done, they don't confess or ever seek forgiveness; we only see blame.

This is not our finest moment, but I am glad God shows us who we are. We are selfish, sinful, and shameful. More often than not, these are our responses to sin: we cover and hide, and blame.

A Good God Responds to Our Sin.

But I don't want to leave with only bad news today. I want you to see something special in this text that we often miss. Following this moment of sin, God hands out punishment for sin to all three parties—man, woman, and the serpent. He does so because God is just. But we cannot miss that God loves man as well, even though man sins.

Genesis 3:21 reads this way:

And the Lord God made for Adam and for his wife garments of skins and clothed them.
Genesis 3:21

I love this one sentence because it demonstrates and implies a number of things. First, it illustrates that God still loves and wants to show compassion for his creation, specifically his finest creation—mankind. Second, we see that God sees the shortcomings of their covering and designs something finer for them—a garment of skin. Third, it is implied that in making this garment of skin that God is willing to aid in covering over their sin and shame through offering a sacrifice of an animal. I believe there is symbolism here that we should not miss. While the text does not explicitly state which animal God sacrificed, I don't think I would be far off in assuming this animal was possibly a lamb used to cover the shame of their sin. So please do miss that God in lieu of our sin, still loves us, and is willing to going to great lengths to pursue us and provide us with hope and a restored relationship with him.

Reflection & Discussion Questions:
- Which of three teachings today on the **bait** of sin, the **rationalization** of sin, and the **response** to sin captured your attention? Is there a specific point that struck you as important for you to know or hear?
- What issue do you need to take in regard to your sin?
- What steps would be important to take immediately?

Call to Action

- Identify a sin you are dealing with in your life and determine one of the points that you think you need to address. Here they are again:
  - Bait one: Questioning the truth
  - Bait two: Twisting the truth
  - Bait three: Desire for more
  - Rationalization one: It's good
  - Rationalization two: It's a delight
  - Rationalization three: It's wisdom
  - Response one: Cover and hide
  - Response two: Blame
- Identify **why** this is an issue for you.
- Identify **what** you need to do about it.

FUNDAMENTAL

6

REAL REPENTANCE

A Moment of Repentance

Today we are going to digging into the meaning and understanding of the word *repentance*.

While this is not a word we commonly use in the English language, Spanish-speaking cultures use this word all the time. *"De repente"* in Spanish means *suddenly*. In ancient Hebrew, which is the language of the Old Testament, this word means *to turn*. The concept is to make an abrupt *about-face* and turn to move in the other direction.

For just a moment, I want you to think back to a significant *turning point* in your spiritual journey. For example, a moment where you made a spiritual *about-face*.

I had one of these moments when I was a young adult. In a previous session, you may remember that reading and memorizing Colossians 3, served a divine purpose in my spiritual life. Well, I will never forget that day as long as I live. I had moved out of my grandparents' home and was living life as I saw best, but all it left me with was a feeling of loneliness. One day I woke up to the realization that my life was not heading down the best path and that something was missing. At this moment, I came enough to my senses to have a short conversation with God. And this is when those words of Colossians 3 came rushing back to me. They came back to me vividly. I just began saying them out loud, even though it had been a few years since I had even touched a Bible. Keep in mind; I had decided that this God thing was a hoax. But these words stirred me enough that I decided I need to give God another chance as if it was me who was going to give him a chance. So in this moment of clarity, I decided that the only right response was to head home—my grandparents' home. The only place I knew to go.

So, I packed everything I owned, which was not much into my truck at the time. It was a 1957 VW Truck. But there was only one issue, the transmission was stuck in second gear, and I was about 150 miles from home. So, I knew I was in for a long trip for this old 36 horsepower motor, by my calculations, that was going to be about 5 hours.

I am cruising down a California freeway going about 25 miles per hour. The RPM's are revving high; the engine is heating up, the heat is on in the cab to pull some of the heat off the engine, the safari windows on the front are open, the wind is blowing on my face when a song from an old poet comes on my transistor radio. His name: Bob Dylan. The song: *"Like a Rolling Stone."* I turned my little radio up loud enough to hear it over the hum of the engine, and the words he sang struck me to the heart. They went like this:

Once upon a time, you dressed so fine
Threw the bums a dime in your prime, didn't you?
People call say 'beware doll, you're bound to fall'
You thought they were all kidding you
You used to laugh about
Everybody that was hanging out
Now you don't talk so loud
Now you don't seem so proud
About having to be scrounging your next meal

How does it feel, how does it feel?
To be without a home
Like a complete unknown, like a rolling stone
Bob Dylan

And fellas, right there in that truck I started weeping like a baby. Nineteen years old, cruising down I-80, the wind blowing in my face, traveling at warp speeds of 20-25 mph, with people flying past me at going 80-90—man, I must have been a scene!

But you know, I really didn't care.

Many hours later, I pulled up in front of my grandfather's home. Everything was fine until this moment when I made that drive down the street. I stopped in front of my grandfather's house and brought my worn-out truck to a stop. I turned the ignition off, but the engine was so worked up that it was gas idling even after turning it off. After I gassed it one last time, it puttered to a stop. I recall sitting in the driver's seat, thinking to myself that there is no way this truck is going to start again.

So, my hand was dealt: I was going to have to make the most challenging walk of my life. It was the walk from my truck to my grandfather's front door. Here's what made it hard: despite my grandfather's love, acceptance, generosity, and mentorship I had spent the last few years living my way and recklessly pursuing my path as I saw fit, not living in obedience to God. And at this moment, I was ashamed of that.

After what seemed like an hour, I finally peeled my sweaty butt from the seat and made the way to the house. As I made my way up the walkway, I saw in the front window that my grandfather was lying back in his old reclining chair. He was taking his usual afternoon nap, with his bald head shining back at me. It was hard to see him sitting there, and guilt and shame overwhelmed me. I wasn't sure if he would accept me or even let me in. But I kept making the walk. I hit that front step and noticed he had vacated his chair, which was now gently rocking. For me, there were about ten steps that ascended to his front door, and as soon as I hit that first step, the front door swung open. There he stood. Smiling. Waiting. Eager. Then he said, seven words I will never forget. He turned his head to the kitchen, where my grandmother was cooking and said:

Grandma, our lost son, has come home.

And then he opened his arms, embraced me, and welcomed me in.

That single moment in my life was the first time I had experienced true love, acceptance, grace, forgiveness, and mercy simultaneously. For me, it was a transformational moment. This moment began a significant turning point in my spiritual life. However, it took me a couple of years to connect what my grandfather said that day on the threshold of his home to the biblical reference he subtly made.

You see, my grandfather was referencing a biblical story: one of repentance. It was perhaps one of the greatest stories Jesus ever told, called the *Story of the Prodigal Son*. What makes this story so great is that Jesus is showing us all what real repentance looks like. You see, repentance is hard to see since its motivational aspects must come from the heart, but when we see the action and experience the results, repentance is breathtaking.

Goal

So, the goal in today's lesson is to define and understand the qualities of real repentance with the hope that we will embrace repentance in our lives.

Pray

God, we need help understanding this great truth. Show us today both what counterfeit and real repentance looks like so that we will make the turn to you. In Christ's name—Amen.

Opener Reflection Questions

- What is one behavior that when other people do it, it drives you crazy?
- When is the last time you heard someone say "sorry," and then you saw them make an "actionable" change as a result?
- What have been one or two behaviors that have been hard for you to change in your spiritual journey that you would love to change permanently?

The Message of Repentance

So let's begin with an interesting fact. Did you know the first word that Jesus preached was the word "*repent*"?

In Matthew chapter 4, we discover that Jesus is about to launch out into his three-year season of ministry. But before he does, he spends 40 days in prayer and fasting. As this time closes off, he is tempted by Devil. Then in Matthew 4, verse 17, we see the message that Jesus is going to preach to the world. Here is how it reads:

From that time Jesus began to preach, saying,
"Repent, for the kingdom of heaven is at hand."
Matthew 4:17

Yep, his first word. *Repent*!

But let's make sure we have a solid understanding of what this word means. So, we can look this up in a Bible Lexicon or Dictionary and discover that this word means:

> *To have a change of self (heart and mind) that abandons former dispositions and results in a new self, new behavior, and regret over former behavior and dispositions.*

Now that's a pretty good definition. You'll notice that repentance means there are multiple things happening in a person all at once: in his mind, heart, motive, and behavior. While this definition is very good, I think Jesus illustrates this even better. In the story of the Prodigal Son, we discover a few main characters. First, we encounter a self-centered younger brother. Second, we encounter a self-righteousness older brother. Third, we encounter a generous, loving, forgiving, and accepting father, who represents God. Right in the middle of this story we see a vivid picture of real repentance.

I want to encourage you to read this story this week, maybe a few times. But here is the essence of it, and then I want to focus in our three verses that will give us the clearest definition and decisive qualities of real repentance.

A Moment of Real Repentance

So the story begins back in Luke 15 verse 1. What is happening is a group of religious leaders are heckling Jesus because he is spending time with men who are so called sinners. So, Jesus tells them a series of stories to help them understand why he's doing this. First, he tells them two quick anecdotal stories. A story about a lost sheep and a one about a lost coin. The principle being, if you had a lost sheep or a lost coin you too would search for it because of its value. Thus Jesus is inferring lost people are valuable to him. But the third story is the one where Jesus really hammers home a point.

The story begins with a loving father who had two sons, and it's the younger son who is the outright rebel. This son decides one day he wants to have nothing to do with his father and demands his inheritance, which is something a father would only do upon death. So this younger son, who has told his father basically, that he wishes he was dead, receives his inheritance and goes his way. He then travels to a distant country, squanders the wealth, and finds himself in a position of utter desperation. He is now doing what no Jewish young man would ever do, he is farming swine. Not just that, he was so hungry and poor, he looked down and the food the pigs were eating and longed to eat it. We would say this young man has pretty much hit "rock bottom."

But it's the next few lines of the story that give us one of the best definitions of repentance in the entire Bible. I think Jesus gives us this story so we have a clear picture of the qualities of real repentance. Here is how the text reads in Luke 15:17-19:

> *"But when **he came to himself**, he said, 'How many of my father's hired servants have more than enough bread, but I perish here with hunger! **I will arise and go** to my father, and I will say to him, "**Father, I have sinned against heaven and before you. I am no longer worthy to be called your son**.***
> *Treat me as one of your hired servants."'*
> **Luke 15:17-19**

You will notice I've underlined a few key phrases in the statement this young man made. Jesus is very intentional about what he said here. We can draw on this text for a very clear understanding of real repentance.

Here are four qualities of real repentance. Quality one is **mental awareness.** Jesus says, *"he came to himself"* or we might say *"he came to his senses."* And thus we see he has an intellectual recognition that something needs to change. Quality two is **changed action**. He takes action. Here is what the text says, *"I will arise and go."* This is another step in real repentance, not just being convicted but acting on that conviction. Quality three, **emotional sorrow**. Now it may be hard to see his emotion in this text, keep in mind this young man is a fictional character, but Jesus definitely infers it. Just listen to the statement the young man has prepared, *"Father, I have sinned against heaven and before you. I am not longer worthy to be called your son."* Without a doubt Jesus is conveying some pretty heartfelt emotion in the turn this young man is making. We can hear his guilt, regret, and shame. No Jew would miss the shame this brought to a family's home. But Jesus intends to emphasize this young man's sense of his own sorrow. Quality four is **sincere motivation**. We see this in his final words, *"Treat me as one of your hired servants."* What the young son is communicating is that he would happily live in father's home without an identity. That he would give up his sonship, identity, and all his rights if he could live again under the shelter and salvation of his father's home. I would say this gives us a look at how sincere this young man is in this moment. That he is sincerely pleading for the mercy of his father in hopes that he will know his genuine motivation.

And thus, in three short verses, within a very descriptive story, Jesus illustrates a definition of repentance. Here are the qualities again. Mental awareness, changed action, emotional sorrow, and sincere motivation.

This is what it means to *"repent"* or *"turn"* in our life. This is what an *"about face"* looks like. It's not just one of these qualities but all four—together. It's something we do with God, in our relationship with him. We turn from our ways toward His way.

Types of Counterfeit Repentance

Even though this is a very good description, I think we can get a better understanding sometimes, when we see a counterfeit product. For example, I can understand the difference between something that genuine and ingenuine when I set them next to each other.

I think we all know that there is some counterfeit repentance in the Christian market today. So for a couple of minutes let's look at what repentance looks like when it is less than genuine. Or when it is missing one of the four qualities above.

One type of counterfeit repentance is what I'll call **Pretending**. This is to give a false appearance of being, possessing, or performing a spiritual act before God and others. An example of this is found in Luke 18:10-14. In this situation, Jesus tells a story of two men who went up to the temple to pray. In the story, he clarifies a contrast between the two. One who is genuine and one who **pretends**. Therefore, while he takes **action**, a quality of repentance, he fails to manifest mental **awareness**, emotional **sorrow**, or sincere **motivation** in what he's doing.

> *"Two men went up into the temple to pray, one a Pharisee and the other a tax collector. The Pharisee, standing by himself, prayed thus: 'God, I thank you that I am not like other men, extortioners, unjust, adulterers, or even like this tax collector. I fast twice a week; I give tithes of all that I get.' But the tax collector, standing far off, would not even lift up his eyes to heaven, but beat his breast, saying, 'God, be merciful to me, a sinner!'*
> **Luke 18:10-14**

A second type of counterfeit repentance is what we call **Regret**. 2 Corinthians 7:10 references this. Here's how it reads:

> *For godly grief produces a repentance that leads to salvation without regret, whereas worldly grief produces death.*
> **2 Corinthians 7:10**

Regret is the type of sorrow we feel for getting caught. It's a worldly regret, not godly or emotional sorrow for what we did and who we hurt.

True emotional sorrow, or *"grief,"* is the word in this text, understands that we have committed a sin and it leads to changed action. When you feel only part of the sorrow (that is the regret for getting caught) but don't have clear mental awareness of the issue, changed action, and sincere motivation then that's counterfeit repentance. Even more we may not have the mental awareness at that point that our sin is affecting other people and even damaging our relationship with God.

A third type of counterfeit repentance is what we call **Blaming**. This is a defense mechanism in a wrong-doing, and it attempts deflect any type of repentance. The most famous illustration of this in the Bible is in Genesis 3:11-13. We read these words in our lesson on sin. Here is how it reads:

> He said, "Who told you that you were naked? Have you eaten of the tree of which I commanded you not to eat?" The man said, "The woman whom you gave to be with me, she gave me fruit of the tree, and I ate." Then the Lord God said to the woman, "What is this that you have done?" The woman said, "The serpent deceived me, and I ate."
>
> **Genesis 3:11-13**

So what we have here is two people, Adam and Eve, caught in the act of sin. God even gives them opportunity to confess their sin and come clean before him, but they both in a moment of self-preservation deflect responsibility, then explain, and even blame—but no hint of repentance. Not even a tiny glimpse of it. I think we are safe to say blaming is not repentance, at all, since it has none of the qualities of repentance. And this is why some people only learn through consequences and pain. God hands out some consequences and punishments to teach repentance.

Reflection & Discussion Questions:
- Which of the counterfeit repentances have you been known to exhibit?
- Which of the four qualities of real repentance do you need to address in becoming more genuine in repentance to God?
- Is there something you need to repent to God today?
- Share it with someone this week and let them pray for you.

Call to Action
- Is there something that you need to repent of in your relationship with God? If so, repent and do a quality check against the four marks of real repentance.
- Want to go to the next level? Share this with a friend and let him pray with you.

FUNDAMENTAL

7

ADVENTUROUS FAITH

It's Faith

Today we are going to be looking at how to live out an adventurous faith, which is what I think most Christian men want. But we need to have a solid understanding of the word: *faith*.

Faith is a word that means to have confidence and trust in a person, thing, or concept. When applied in a Christian context, it infers supreme confidence in the person of God and his word and promises.

There are several texts in the bible that give us an excellent understanding of what this means. The first the Hebrews 11:1. It gives us both a definition of faith right before it lists many examples of people who lived with adventurous faith. Here's how it reads:

Now faith is the assurance of things hoped for, the conviction of things not seen.
Hebrews 11:1

There are two very descriptive words in this text: *assurance* and *conviction*. These words suggest that faith has this objective certainty that is immovable. But the objective certainty is in something that is less than tangible. In fact, it's *unseen*. While this sounds a little bit paradoxical, it is not. In the section of scripture that follows Hebrews 11:1, the author lists a lot of evidence of what this *assurance and confidence in the unseen* looks like. This chapter is called by some the great Hall of Faith and listed here are men and women who acted with faith.

So the next question becomes, how do we build this supreme confidence and objective certainty?

Well, another verse will offer us a lot of guidance. It's Romans 10:17. It reads:

So faith comes from hearing, and hearing through the word of Christ.
Romans 10:17

While faith is challenging, God makes it a little easier for us. He does this by revealing direction through his word. His word, spoken over time, has been revealed by him in the bible, and also in the person and the work of Jesus Christ. It is hearing his word and listening to Jesus that strengthens our faith, one day at a time. Over a lifetime, we grow in confidence in him.

But this move from human confidence to spiritual confidence takes time. The only thing that stands in our way of us making progress in faith is this one thing: *fear*.

Debilitating Fear

Now I don't know about you, but I have fears. And I would assume you have a few as well.

For example, I have a couple of long-time trivial human fears. One of them is a fear of deep water. Now I'll go snorkeling and have even gone scuba diving. But the whole idea of being in deep water and not being able to see above, below, or behind me is frightening to me. As a non-amphibious creature, my eyes only give me forward vision, and therefore I believe I was made to stand on solid ground, not navigate a world where large fish can outswim and attack me from behind. Yes, I am one of those guys, who is entertained by Shark Week, but I don't want to be put in the water with them.

Now, this fear is a little trivial, but we also have real fears, some that are even debilitating that are based on real experiences and events in our life.

For example, several years ago, my daughter and I were in a severe car accident. Traveling at 70 mph down a dark interstate at about midnight on Christmas Eve, we hit a patch of black ice on the freeway, and we spun out. We ended up T-boning a guard rail on an overpass, flew about 30 yards in the air, rotated three times down a hill until we came to a stop in a dark ditch near some railroad tracks. We hit that guardrail so hard that the shoes on our feet were ejected. Everything, yes everything, was ejected from the vehicle—except us. We both walked away from the accident, sore and in shock. Yet for months, if not years, my driving habits on icy days drastically changed. And why? Fear. Our fears have both a good-side and a dark-side to it.

For many, human fear is debilitating. Fear, in combination with a significant event, will alter how we think, feel, and behave. On our spiritual journey, we encounter these fearful moments. We may not talk about them, but they happen. They are moments of human fear that lead to hesitancy in the adventure of faith. Yet if we can learn to unlearn these learned responses, we can develop some supreme confidence and objective certainty—becoming great men of great faith.

Goal
So, the goal in today's lesson is to discover how fear and faith oppose adventurous faith and, at the same time, launch us into it, with the outcome of identifying a place where you might need to take a leap of faith in your relationship with Jesus Christ.

Pray
God, help me to understand my fears so that I can live in greater faith today, and every day. In Christ's name—Amen.

Opener Reflection Questions
- What is one fear you have?
- Why do you fear this? Try to explain where you think this fear comes from.
- Have you taken steps to overcome this fear? Describe what you've done.

Let's Go for a Walk
We are going to dig into a famous New Testament story. It's the account of Jesus and Peter and their walk on water. I know for some of you, this may be a familiar, but I am hoping today that you'll observe something new from this text that will decrease your fear and increase faith in Jesus Christ.

So, here is the set up for this moment. Jesus has just spent an entire day performing extraordinary miracles. As the day draws to a close, there were now over 5000 people gathered and hungry. Rather than send these men, women, and children home, Jesus feeds them with a few loaves and fishes that they scrounge up from a couple of people. And miraculously, everyone is very well fed.

Then here is what happens in Matthew 14:

Immediately he made the disciples get into the boat and go before him to the other side, while he dismissed the crowds. And after he had dismissed the crowds, he went up on the mountain by himself to pray. When evening came, he was there alone, but the boat by this time was a long way from the land, beaten by the waves, for the wind was against them. And in the fourth watch of the night, he came to them, walking on the sea. But when the disciples saw him walking on the sea, they were terrified, and said, "It is a ghost!" and they cried out in fear. But immediately, Jesus spoke to them, saying, "Take heart; it is I. Do not be afraid."

And Peter answered him, "Lord, if it is you, command me to come to you on the water." He said, "Come." So Peter got out of the boat and walked on the water and came to Jesus. But when he saw the wind, he was afraid, and beginning to sink he cried out, "Lord, save me." Jesus immediately reached out his hand and took hold of him, saying to him, "O you of little faith, why did you doubt?" And when they got into the boat, the wind ceased. And those in the boat worshiped him, saying, "Truly you are the Son of God."
Matthew 14:22-33

A Few Observations

I want to make a few observations. But let's begin with the setting, because the setting of this moment is essential. I want you to imagine a charming lake area encircled by large rolling hills. On the scene, you have men who are experienced sailors. Guys who've been on this lake perhaps hundreds of times during their life. They know the lake, the intended direction, and the vessel well.

The issue they encounter is that they aren't making progress because they are sailing against elements, the waves and wind are persisting against them. In the Gospel of John, we read a similar rendering of the story and learn that they were about 3 miles from shore.

The plot thickens, as we discover they in obedience were rowing all night long without making any real gain toward the goal. This means they got into the boat at around sunset and we find them still in the middle of the lake the next morning between 3-6 AM (which is the fourth watch of the night).

This means we can infer that these men were exhausted and frustrated. At least I know I would be if I had been rowing all through the night. This is a rough estimate, but that's about 12 hours of sailing and rowing in relatively small aquatic vessel.

But notice that Jesus intentionally waits, it's not accidental. If you turn to the Gospel of Mark, you discover in this account that Jesus could see them as he was praying from the mountainside. I would say Jesus is pretty intentional.

So next, let's notice the main characters. There are a few. Jesus, of course is the main character. So is Peter. But we could also say the storm is a central character in this story, since a lot of the story's action is dependent on it, including the water, wind, and waves.

Also, next, let's notice that Peter does some pretty unusual things. Maybe he is just delusional from rowing on that boat for the entire night, but here is what he does. First, he speaks to a premonition on the water. I would say that's a bit odd. Second, he makes a strange request that is going to put his life in danger. Now maybe he just had enough of the storm, but again this is another odd response. Third, he gets out of the boat when Jesus says only one word, "Come." This is crazy, fellas. There is not one person I know, including me, that would do this. In fact, there were a few disciples still on the boat that didn't that probably thought he was crazy. And yet, Peter did it. He did something no other human being did until that moment and has not done since: he walked on water. At least for a little bit. Which is pretty cool when you think about it?

Then there is a sudden turn in the story. It's in verse 30 we read, *"But when he saw the wind, he was afraid."* Thus, everything turns for the worse. But notice what he saw—it's important. He saw the wind. Or more accurately, he saw the effects of the wind, since no one sees the wind. In this split second his attention is diverted from Jesus to what's happening around him. The storm becomes more objective and certain than his walk of faith on the water, and thus he begins to sink. But Peter is not without hope, for the Savior does what he does best—he saves. And then *"immediately"* (I love the use of the adverb here) Jesus reaches out his hand to save him. I can see Jesus smiling in excitement for Peter saying, with a voice of encouragement, not shame, *"O you of little faith, why did you doubt."* Then they walk to the boat together, on water nonetheless, and the wind comes to a sudden halt.

The Object of Fear and Faith

This is great story that makes a fantastic point. But before we get to the point, I want you to consider a very thought-provoking question.

Why is it that we so easily quickly all the amazing things God does in life?

These men on this boat, just witnessed one of the great miracles of all time. Jesus just fed an impossible amount of people with a few fish and a few loaves of bread. A crowd of thousands upon thousands were saved from hunger and slept well fed that night, and then only hours later the same disciples who witnessed that miracle are desperate for the next miracle. While you'd think one miracle would be enough to fortify their faith, it was apparently wasn't.

For example, at the beginning of our time today I mentioned a very significant moment in my life when God saved me and my daughter from certain death in a tragic car accident. While God did something miraculous for us, I spent the next year driving around in fear in concern for my life. Why? Because we quickly forget the lesson of faith.

Here's the deal, and the fantastic point of the story. These men witnessed miracle after miracle, but Jesus's reason for performing the miracles was to help them develop a faith in God. He wants them to overcome their human fears and move from **human fear** to **holy fear**.

You see fear is really not our foe, it's our friend. But it's who or what we fear that makes all the difference. For it's the thing we fear that determines the object of faith. For example, Peter, in this instance, briefly experienced a **holy fear** and thus had a once in a lifetime experience. He became the only man, besides Jesus, to walk on water. I can see him excitedly walking with his eyes locked on Jesus. But there was that tragic moment he *saw the wind* and in this split second his fear changes. It moves from holy fear that was fixed on Jesus to human fear and concern for his own life. Trusting no longer in Jesus but in his human ability, he begins to sink, and what was formerly possible is no longer.

I think this is a big reason why we miss out on the adventure of faith. We spend our lives focused on natural fears, living by our strength, rather than focused on Jesus in holy fear and thus in the adventure of supernatural faith.

Learning to Take Steps of Faith

Here are some real practical steps we can take, and lessons we learn from Peter.

The first step out of the boat begins with **assessing your human and holy fear**.

Notice that Jesus tells Peter precisely what to do, *"Take heart, it is I. Do not be afraid."* Jesus is giving Peter real-world advice. He acknowledges that Peter has real human fears: fear of sinking, failure, and death. Yet Jesus also understands there is a greater fear—holy fear of the One who stands before him on the water, a God who stands before him doing something humanly impossible.

When we encounter fear, it's okay to identify and name the human fears we have. They are after all real fears. But then we should also assess the courage we need and identify the holy fear God wants us to have. For each of us this will be different. This might look like:

- *Standing up for a biblical conviction—which addresses a fear of confrontation.*
- *Living with godly character—which addresses the fear of rejection.*
- *Addressing an impure compulsion—which addresses the fear of change.*
- *Developing a godly discipline—which addresses the fear of taking spiritual action.*

But just consider the benefit on other side of these human fears. They guide us toward holy fear and increased *conviction, character, purity,* and *discipline* which for each of us help us to get out of the boat in faith, trusting more in Jesus Christ in our *"walk on water"* experience.

The second step out getting out of the boat in faith is, **test the object of faith**.

I love that Peter asks the question, *"Lord, if it is you, command me to come to you on the water."* While Peter is a little impulsive throughout the gospels, he also exercises some wisdom here.

He wants a little more evidence. He's looking for that confirmation. He wants to know that it's God's voice. We should do the same.

The best way to test the object of our faith is to confirm it with the bible and the teaching of Jesus Christ. If you have not done this in the past this is the most effective way to unlearn trusting in yourself and addressing human fears. God will always confirm what he wants from us through his word. He will never contradict himself and he is eager even to give us direction.

It's good to pray and ask God for direction. He will confirm this through godly people, his word, and even through circumstance.

The third step in getting out of the boat in faith is, to actually get out of the boat **by taking action**.

Now here's what makes this tricky, taking a leap off the boat could involve action but it could involve inaction. For example, sometimes God will want us to get out of the boat by taking a leap toward godly action. Other times God will want us to get out of the boat not engaging in ungodly action. There are times for both. Both are challenging.

But this is where the adventure begins. The adventure into the unknown. Too many men wait too long to do this and live a life convicted about change and never discover the conviction of acting the change. The key is to act.

Fourth, when you fail in the action, which will happen, **reach out for Jesus' hand**. The Savior loves to save a man who acts in faith, just as he did Peter. So, remember you are going to fail sometimes. But failure when acting in faith, does not mean the Savior dislikes us or disowns us. In fact, you may fail a lot when taking some first steps in faith. Peter did! It's better to fail and learn another way than to never act at all.

Reflection & Discussion Questions:
- Where do you need to take action in your spiritual life? (Identify a godly action you need to start).
- Where do you need to take inaction in your spiritual life? (Identify an ungodly action you need to stop).

- What do you need to do to begin today?

Call to Action

- Share below the action or inaction you are going to take this week.

FUNDAMENTAL

8

SALVATION'S STORY

The Great Story

I think we all love a great story. Great stories have a few components. They have great characters, a fantastic setting, a straightforward plot, and tension created by conflict, and finally resolution. The Bible has all of this and so much more.

The Bible is filled with love, war, birth, and death. It reveals to us an ancient culture, one rich with poetry, history, philosophy, and science. The Bible combines mystery, romance, suspense, thriller, action, and adventure, and it even has a book with a strong parental advisory because of its explicit sexual content.

The Bible has things to say about money. It has something to say about some of the hottest controversies of our time. Politics, government, and the church: the Bible dives into conversation topics you avoid at your Thanksgiving table. It is full of hundreds of prophecies that came true. It is full of scientific ideas that brilliant people are still discovering. It describes many archeological artifacts that we are still trying to find and plenty that we already have. In 1455 it became the first book ever printed on the printing press, and today it continues to be the best-selling and most distributed book of all time, with an estimated 5 billion copies sold. New copies are being produced at a volume of about 100 million each year.

But given all this, we sometimes miss the beauty of the metanarrative, which is the greatest story ever told. Put simply; we need to know the story.

Goal

So, the goal in today's lesson is to learn the story—the story of man's salvation. With the outcome of being able to share this story, the greatest ever told.

Pray

God, as we take a look at your story. The one you have been telling about your son and us, help us to see it, know it and remember it. In Christ's name—Amen.

Opener Reflection Questions

- List a few highlights of your spiritual story?
- If you were asked to tell the story of salvation from the Bible, what points would you make, or what information would you share?

Prepared with the Gospel

I want to begin today with a verse. One that might make you feel a little unprepared today. It's from 1 Peter 3, verse 15; it reads:

But in your hearts honor Christ the Lord as holy, always being prepared to make a defense to anyone who asks you for a reason for the hope that is in you.
1 Peter 3:15

Yep, I told you.

Every time I read this, I feel a little tension about being prepared. Honestly, I am not sure anyone is fully prepared in the way they want to be. But we can take some action to prepare a little bit more every day. I think this lesson will do just that.

The Gospel story is, after all, the greatest story ever told, and it is the reason we are having this conversation right now. Let me say that again, we are here, right now, because someone else, at some point, understood and clearly explained to us the gospel story, and we got it. Fellas, we should be able to do the same. You should be able to do the same. It's not just your pastor's job. It's your job. That's not a guilt trip; it's an essential part of being a follower of Jesus Christ.

But before we dig in, I want to decrypt a critical word that we use to describe the story: it's the word *gospel*.

For some of us, this word is a little unusual because it's an old word. It a descriptor we don't use very often. It's an almost exclusively Christian word. But in the first century, this word's literal meaning was "good news." It was a word someone used when they were bringing a story of "good news" to a king or someone in high authority. Remember: very few people would bring a story of bad news to a king, or they would get their head chopped off. No joke. So bringing the gospel to the king was something to celebrate.

We, too, have a gospel story to tell. It's a story of good news for the world that our King gave to us to share with others. It's not one we share with our King, but that the King shares with us.

We need to be able to explain what is good about Christ that the world needs to hear. This means we have to be able to effectively and efficiently tell the story. Over the years, numerous teachers have simplified this so that we can easily commit it memory and thus share the core of it when needed. In business, we call this an *elevator speech*, and I think this captures the essence of what we are going to do today.

The Romans Road Tells the Story

Now there are many methods to telling the gospel story. But I think a straightforward approach is what some call the Romans Road. Now please note what I am calling the Romans Road is not a literal road. It's a journey through the book of Romans.

The book of Romans, in only four verses, provides a clear understanding of four major parts in the gospel story without having to flip around the entire Bible. The stops on this figurative "road" illustrate the villain, the problem, the hero, and the response.

I think the verses are simple enough that they are easy to memorize. Keep in mind as I reference these verses that I am focusing on specific words in the verses because they make and tell the points of the story.

So here are the four stops on the Romans Road.

STOP ONE: ROMANS 3:23—THE VILLAIN

> ***For all*** *have **sinned** and fall sort of the glory of God.*
> **Romans 3:23**

This first verse tells us about the problem and the villain in the story. Notice the words I've underlined.

First, the words *"for all."* This tells us that *everyone,* which is pretty all-inclusive, who has ever lived or will live, is without exception here.

Second, notice the word *"sinned."* As we discussed in a previous lesson, this is a Christian word that means to *miss the mark* by not living the obedient to God's way in our life.

So what we learn from this first stop on the Romans Roads is that everyone falls short because of sin. This results in us missing what God intended for us to experience of his glory. Now the plot is set.

STOP TWO: ROMANS 6:23—THE PROBLEM & RESULT

---

*For the **wages** of sin is **death**.*
Romans 6:23

Again, another simple and easy to memorize verse. Notice we went from Romans 3:23 to Romans 6:23. But in addition to telling us the problem of sin, we discover the tragic result of sin as well.

The first word I want you to notice in this text is *wage.* Now a wage is something we *earn* and, as a result, *deserve* as payment. For example, when you work, you earn a wage, and you are deserved this wage upon completion of your work.

But the spiritual wage for sin is *death.* This second word that I am highlighting is the bad news of the gospel story. As with any story, you cannot have good news without bad news. But the bad news is *death.* This assumes irreversible consequences, both *physical* and *spiritual.* We all know that we will all die a physical death, but the results of this verse are concerned about *spiritual death.* Spiritual death is permanent separation from God that results in spending an eternity in hell. I don't think there is any worse news than this. Now the plot is set. All that is left is a Savior and salvation, which takes us to our next stop on the Romans Road.

STOP THREE: ROMANS 5:8–THE HERO & HIS SOLUTION

> But **God** shows his love for us in that while we were still sinners, **Christ** **died for us**.
> **Romans 5:8**

Now at stop three, we are getting to some good news. Notice the characters *"God"* and *"Christ"* Now, we have our lead characters and the hero of the story. God sees our hopeless position and knows the impossibility of our conquering sin and death. Even though our sin separates us from him, He extends love to us and provides an escape from sin and the wages we earned in sin. God sent His Son to rescue us from this state of despair.

This leads to the next key phrase, which is the action of the hero in the story; he *"died for us."* Jesus, who lived a pure and holy life without sin, stepped in to pay the wages we earned with his life. Thus he pays off the debt we earned for our sin. He died as a payment for the penalty of our sin. Here, we see that Jesus is God's loving redemption for all people who could not rescue themselves.

STOP FOUR: ROMANS 10:9–THE RESPONSE

> Because, if you **confess** with your mouth that **Jesus is Lord** and **believe** in your heart
> that God **raised him from the dead**, you will be saved.
> **Romans 10:9**

With stop four, we discover our response.

First, notice the word: *confess*. When we confess, we are agreeing or acknowledging something verbally. In this case, we agree that *Jesus is Lord*. This is the second phrase to notice in this text. Jesus' lordship is something a follower proudly acknowledges. We no longer lead our life, but in this confession, Jesus becomes our life leader. Jesus becomes our Lord. We relinquish control to him, and he dictates what we think and what we do.

Third, notice the word *believe*. Believing is the action of our faith. We believe in our heart genuinely and at the deepest level in this fourth and final phrase—that God *raised him from the dead.* The resurrection is the linchpin to everything in our faith. The Christian faith celebrates two important miracles that substantiate our belief. First, the birth of Jesus and second his resurrection from the dead—Christmas and Easter. But the resurrection is proof that God has the power to defeat both types of death. Both physical death and spiritual death are overcome by him so that we could have spiritual life and a renewed relationship with God.

Okay, I know this is a lot of information, but it's just four verses:

Romans 3:23, Romans 6:23, Romans 5:8, and Romans 10:9. Four stops on the Romans Road, and remember the verses tell the story! (And it's easy to memorize.)

Reflection & Discussion Questions:
- Was there a moment or moments in your life that came to mind while reading through the Roman's Road? Why did this come to mind?
- How is God's Story also your story?
- Is there someone today, you might want to pray for that does not know salvation's story.

Call to Action
- Memorize Romans 3:23, Romans 6:23, Romans 5:8, and Romans 10:9.
- Want to go further? Share the gospel story with someone you know.